GUIDEBOOK
FOR
CONFESSION
FOR
CHILDREN

(FROM 9-13 YEARS OLD)

Edited by Beatriz B. Brillantes

SINAG-TALA
PUBLISHERS, INC.
Manila

GUIDEBOOK FOR CONFESSION FOR CHILDREN
© 1987 by Sinag-tala Publishers, Inc.
Edited by Beatriz B. Brillantes
Illustrations and Art Design by Ma. Teresa Uson-Manas
   and Zumra dela Cruz

Nihil Obstat: Msgr. Benedicto Aquino
                Second Vice-Chancellor

Imprimatur :   Msgr. Josefino S. Ramirez
                Chancellor
                July 1987

First Philippine printing, August 1987

ISBN: 971-117-038-8

SINAG-TALA PUBLISHERS, INC.
Greenhills P.O. Box 536
Manila 3113, Philippines

CONTENTS

Sin is disobedience to God

Sin is doing something bad. We say it is bad because it is disobeying God. It is something that God does not like. It is a bad thought, a bad word, a bad action, or not doing the good we must do.

God punishes sin. There are big sins and little sins. God punishes the big sins in hell. God punishes the little sins in purgatory.

We commit a big sin when we are sure something is VERY BAD but are willing to do it.

We commit a little sin when we are willing to do something bad, but honestly believe it is NOT VERY BAD.

There are big sins and little sins. Mortal sins are big sins, and they take away the life of grace from us. If we die with mortal sin, we go to hell.

The other kind of sin is called venial. They are very small sins which do not take away the life of grace, but still they displease God.

God wants us to be His good children. If we disobey Him, we make Him sad. SIN IS DISOBEDIENCE TO GOD'S LAWS.

GOD NEVER LIKES SIN, BIG OR SMALL.

It is only the devil who likes sin.

Mortal sin makes us:

1. lose sanctifying grace
   — God's love;
2. lose our right to heaven;
3. lose all our good works; and
4. unable to do anything for heaven.

Venial sins:

1. makes us love God less;
2. makes us less worthy of God's help; and
3. weakens us against mortal sin.

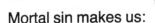

WHAT DOES GOD WANT YOU TO DO?

1. I should pray to God and love Him above all things.

2. I should love God's Holy Name and all holy persons and things.

3. I should go to Mass on Sundays and Holy days, and do no unnecessary work on those days.

4. I should love and obey my parents and those who have charge over me.

5. I should be kind to everybody.

6. I should be pure in all I do.

7. I should not steal.

8. I should not tell lies.

9. I should be pure in my thoughts.

10. I should not wish to cheat or steal.

A father had two sons. One son said: "I don't want to work at home any more. Give me my money, so I can go away." The father gave the money to the son. Then the son went far away. He did many bad things. He wasted his money. Soon he was very poor, and he had to watch pigs in the pasture and share their food. He was very hungry and unhappy.

Then he thought of his many sins, and he became very sad.

He said to himself: "I will go home to my father and ask him to forgive me, and let me work for him again." He went home.

The father saw the son coming home. So he ran out to meet the son and embraced him. The son wept and said "Father, I have sinned. I am sorry. Please forgive me. Now I promise to be good and work for you always as your servant. The father was very happy and said "I forgive you." He prepared a big feast for him to show his happiness.

The parable shows that God is full of mercy toward those who ask pardon for their sins. Like the father of the prodigal son, he welcomes them with open arms and great joy.

Confession is telling our sins to a priest to obtain forgiveness. We go to the priest who takes Christ's place and Christ through the priest, forgives our sins.

IS IT NECESSARY TO CONFESS EVERY SIN?

It is necessary to confess every mortal sin which has not yet been confessed and forgiven; it is not necessary to confess our venial sins but it is better to do so. Children rarely have mortal sins to confess, but venial sins are frequent. To grow in love of God, we should confess every venial sin that we can remember.

WHAT DO WE DO IF WITHOUT OUR FAULT WE FORGET TO CONFESS OUR MORTAL SIN?

If without our fault, we forget to confess a mortal sin, we may receive Holy Communion, because the sin is forgiven; but we must tell the sin if it comes to our mind again.

WHAT MUST I DO IF I KNOWINGLY KEEP BACK A MORTAL SIN IN CONFESSION?

A person who has knowingly kept back a mortal sin in confession must confess that he has made a bad confession, tell the sin he has kept back, and mention the sacraments he has received since that time.

1

BEFORE CONFESSION

- *It is easy to go to confession.*
- *Do not be afraid. The priest is ready to help you.*
- *Know all your sins before you see the priest.*
  If there is something that you do not know how to tell, say to the priest: "Father, I have something to say, but I do not know exactly how to say it. Please help me."
- *Kneel properly and keep your hands and feet still.*

9

DURING CONFESSION

- *Whisper loud enough for the priest to hear your sins. Only he should hear them.*

- *Don't make him ask you after each sin, "<u>how many times</u>?" Tell him!*

- *Don't make him ask you, over and over again, "<u>What else</u>?" Tell him!*

  Continue talking until you have told everything.

3

AFTER CONFESSION

- *After you finish telling all your sins, say:*
  "That is all, Father, I am sorry for all my sins."

- *Then listen to him. He may ask questions. Be able to answer them honestly.*

- *He may also teach you what to do to avoid sin and to do better.*

- *He may show you how you can love Jesus more each day.*

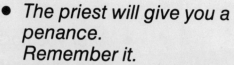

- *The priest will give you a penance.*
  Remember it.
- *The penance is a prayer or a good work that you do to show God that you are very sorry for your sins.*
- *The priest then gives the absolution. This is Jesus Himself forgiving your sins.*
- *While the priest gives the absolution, say the Act of Contrition slowly and devoutly.*

> Penance is the sacrament through which Jesus pardons all our sins committed after baptism. It is also called the Sacrament of Reconciliation.
> Penance is also the prayer or good work that you do to show God that you are very sorry for your sins.

To receive the sacrament of Penance, we tell our sins to the priest in confession.

In the sacrament of Penance, the priest stands for our Lord Jesus Christ.

The priest and the person who is confessing take part with Jesus Christ in the Sacrament of Penance. The most important part is taken by Jesus Christ. He takes over in confession.

When do we receive the sacrament of Penance?

We receive the sacrament of Penance when we made a good confession and we receive the words of absolution from the priest.

13

What are the elements needed to make a good confession?

There are few steps to a good confession. Here are five steps to a good confession:

1. EXAMINE YOUR CONSCIENCE.
2. BE SORRY FOR YOUR SINS.
3. RESOLVE NEVER TO COMMIT THEM AGAIN.
4. TELL YOUR SINS TO THE PRIEST.
5. SAY OR DO YOUR PENANCE.

Remembering that it is Our Lord Himself to whom we are confessing our sins helps us to be very sincere and very sorry.

1
EXAMINE YOUR CONSCIENCE

I SHALL THINK OF MY FAULTS. I SHOULD KNOW WHAT FAULTS I HAVE TO TELL THE PRIEST IN CONFESSION. I SHOULD KNOW HOW MANY TIMES I COMMITTED EACH ONE.

15

- DID I MISBEHAVE OR HAVE AN IMPROPER POSTURE OR DRESS IN CHURCH OR CAUSE OTHERS TO GET DISTRACTED?

- DID I ANSWER BACK MY PARENTS AND TEACHERS?

- DO I DO MY HOUSE CHORES?

- DID I EAT OR DRINK MORE THAN THE SUFFICIENT AMOUNT, ALLOWING MYSELF TO GET CARRIED AWAY BY GLUTTONY?

- AM I SELFISH IN THE USE OF MY POSSESSIONS ?

- DOES IT HURT ME TO SHARE THEM WITH MY BROTHERS AND SISTERS ?

- DID I MISS MASS ON SUNDAY OR HOLY DAYS OF OBLIGATION OR ARRIVE LATE SO AS NOT TO FULFIL THE PRECEPTS ?

- DID I EASILY GET ANGRY OR LOSE MY TEMPER ?

- AM I DILIGENT IN MY WORK AND STUDIES OR DO I GIVE IN TO LAZINESS OR LOVE OF COMFORT?

- DO I FORGIVE MY ENEMIES?

- DID I NEGLECT TO PAY MY DEBT?

- DID I HELP OTHERS IN THEIR WORKS OR STUDY, OR DID I HINDER THEM SOME WAY, BY DISTRACTING THEM, CAUSING THEM DISCOURAGEMENT, INTERRUPTIONS, ETC.?

- DID I READ BAD BOOKS OR LOOK AT IMMODEST PICTURES? DID I GO TO IMMODEST SHOWS?

- DID I ENGAGE IN IMPURE CONVERSATIONS? DID I START THEM?

- DID I CAUSE ANYONE HARM WITH MY WORDS OR ACTIONS? DO I PARDON WHENEVER I OFFEND ANYONE? DID I CALL ANYONE NAMES? DO I INSULT OR TEASE OTHERS?

- DID I LEAD OTHERS TO SINS OF IMPURITY OR IMMODESTY? WHAT SIN?

- DO I LIKE TO KEEP BAD THOUGHTS IN MY MIND?

- DID I SPEND BEYOND MY MEANS? DO I SPEND TOO MUCH MONEY UNNECESSARILY DUE TO WHIM, VANITY OR CAPRICE?

- DID I STEAL ANY OBJECT OR AMOUNT OF MONEY? DID I GIVE IT BACK? OR AT LEAST, HAVE THE INTENTION TO DO SO?

- DID I GO WITH BAD COMPANIONS?

• DO I GIVE ALMS ACCORDING TO MY CAPACITY?

• DO I INSULT OR TEASE OTHERS?

• AM I ENVIOUS OF MY NEIGHBOR'S GOODS?

• WAS I GREEDY? DO I HAVE AN EXCESSIVELY MATERIALISTIC VIEW OF LIFE?

- DO I RECITE MY USUAL PRAYERS IN THE MORNING AND BEFORE GOING TO BED?

- DID I RECEIVE HOLY COMMUNION IN THE STATE OF MORTAL SIN OR WITHOUT THE NECESSARY PREPARATION?

- DID I MISS THE ONE-HOUR EUCHARISTIC FAST?

- DID I FAIL TO MENTION OUT OF EMBARRASSMENT SOME GRAVE SIN IN MY PREVIOUS CONFESSION?

- DID I READ BOOKS, PAMPHLETS OR MAGAZINES CONTRARY TO THE CATHOLIC FAITH?

- DID I SAY BAD WORDS?

- WAS I LAZY?

- DID I ALLOW MYSELF TO BE DISTRACTED BY NOT PAYING ATTENTION, LOOKING AROUND OUT OF CURIOSITY, ETC.?

- DO I TELL LIES?

- HAVE I JUSTLY ACCUSED OTHERS?

- DID I TELL THE FAULTS OF OTHERS WITHOUT NECESSITY?

- DID I REVEAL SECRETS WITHOUT DUE CAUSE?

2
BE SORRY FOR YOUR SINS

NOW, I MUST BE SORRY FOR THEM. I MUST MAKE UP MY MIND NOT TO BE BAD AGAIN. MY CONFESSION WILL NOT BE GOOD IF I AM NOT SORRY.

PRAYERS BEFORE CONFESSION

- *My dear Jesus, I wish to make a good confession. Please help me to be truly sorry for all my sins. I am sorry, from my heart.*

- *My dear Jesus, I am sorry, because I know that you must punish me for my sins.*

- *My dear Jesus, I am sorry, because sin made you suffer and die upon the cross.*

- *My dear Jesus, I love you. You are so good and kind to me. My sins hurt your Sacred Heart. I hate them! I shall never commit them again.*

RESOLVE NEVER TO COMMIT THEM AGAIN

I AM SORRY FOR MY FAULTS IF I CAN TRULY SAY, "I WISH I HAD NEVER COMMITTED THEM. I WISH I COULD TAKE THEM BACK. I WILL NOT DISPLEASE JESUS AGAIN." SO WHEN I KNOW ALL THE WRONG I HAVE DONE, I KNEEL DOWN AND TALK TO JESUS.

I WILL GLADLY MAKE LITTLE SACRIFICES TO PROVE MY LOVE FOR JESUS. I WILL BE KIND TO OTHERS. I WILL TRY TO FOLLOW HIS EXAMPLE. "YOU DIED FOR LOVE OF US, MY GOOD JESUS. O JESUS, FORGIVE ME MY SINS! I WILL ALWAYS BE YOUR LOVING CHILD. I WANT YOU TO BE HAPPY. HELP ME TO BE GOOD!"

NOW, I AM READY TO GO TO CONFESSION. I DO NOT WORRY EVEN IF I CANNOT REMEMBER EVERYTHING. JESUS DOES NOT MIND IF I REALLY FORGET. HE KNOWS HOW EASY IT IS FOR ME TO FORGET.

BUT FIRST I SAY AN ACT OF CONTRITION. THIS IS A PRAYER TELLING GOD THAT I AM SORRY I HAVE HURT HIM.

AN ACT OF CONTRITION

O my God, I am heartily sorry for having offended You, and I detest all my sins because I dread the loss of heaven and the pains of hell, but most of all because they offended You, my God, Who are all good and deserving of all my love. I firmly resolve with the help of Your grace, to confess my sins, to do penance, and to amend my life. Amen.

Or I can say,

"O my God, I am sorry for all my sins, because they displease You, Who are all good and deserving of all my love. With your help, I will sin no more."

This is a shorter version of the act of contrition.

Next I go into the confessional and kneel. I wait until the priest opens the little window.

I say: "This is my first confession." If I have gone to confession before, I say: "It has been one week (or one month) since my last confession."

Now I must tell how many times I committed each fault.

If I have done something that I do not know how to tell, I say, "Father, I have a fault but I do not know how to say it." The priest will help me.

When I have told all my sins, I say, "I am sorry for all my sins. That is all, Father."

AFTER I HAVE TOLD ALL MY FAULTS, THE PRIEST TELLS ME HOW TO BE A BETTER CHILD. I LISTEN VERY WELL.

THEN HE TELLS ME TO DO SOMETHING OR TO SAY SOME PRAYERS. THIS IS MY PENANCE. IT IS A SMALL PENALTY FOR MY SINS.

LAST OF ALL, THE PRIEST TELLS ME TO SAY THE ACT OF CONTRITION. THEN HE MAKES THE SIGN OF THE CROSS OVER ME. THIS MEANS GOD IS TAKING AWAY ALL MY SINS. GOD IS MAKING MY SOUL ALL BEAUTIFUL AGAIN.

AS THE PRIEST MAKES THE SIGN OF THE CROSS OVER ME, I ALSO MAKE THE SIGN OF THE CROSS. AFTER THIS, I FEEL CLOSE TO JESUS AGAIN.

I DO NOT GO AWAY UNTIL THE PRIEST CLOSES THE LITTLE WINDOW. THEN I GO BACK TO MY SEAT. I KNEEL DOWN AND SAY MY PENANCE.

THEN I THANK GOD FOR MY CONFESSION.

29

PRAYER AFTER CONFESSION

My dear Jesus, I thank You for being so good to me. I promise to try hard not to fall again into sin.

My dear Jesus, I remember all Your sufferings. I am sorry! My sins caused it all. Please teach me to hate and to fear sin.

My dear Jesus, teach me to love You!

If I love You, I shall always try to please You.

My Mother Mary, help me to thank Jesus for His kindness to me.

I have been to confession. I have told all my sins. I promise to be good and to flee from the least sin.

Please watch over me and protect me.

My Guardian Angel, be ever at my side, to keep sin far away from me.

WHAT ARE THE CHIEF QUALITIES OF A GOOD CONFESSION?

8

> The chief qualities of a good confession are three: it must be humble, sincere and entire.

NO EXCUSES   **NO FALSEHOODS**   **NO OMISSIONS**

HUMBLE   **SINCERE**   **ENTIRE**

When is our confession humble?

Our confession is humble when we accuse ourselves of our sins with a conviction of guilt for having offended God.

When is our confession sincere?

Our confession is sincere when we tell our sins honestly and frankly.

31

When is our confession entire?

Our confession is entire when we confess at least all our mortal sins, telling their kind, the number of times we have committed each sin, and any circumstances changing their nature.

What are we to do if without our fault we forget to confess a mortal sin?

If without our fault we forget to confess a mortal sin, we may receive Holy Communion, because we have made a good confession and the sin is forgiven; but we must tell the sin in confession if it again comes to our mind.

What happens if we knowingly conceal a mortal sin in confession?

If we knowingly conceal a mortal sin in confession, the sins we confess are not forgiven; moreover, we commit a mortal sin of sacrilege.

What must a person who has knowingly concealed a mortal sin in confession do?

A person who has knowingly concealed a mortal sin in confession must confess that he has made a bad confession, tell the sin he has concealed, mention the sacraments he has received since that time, and confess all the mortal sins he has committed since his last confession.

John has four
mortal sins.

He goes to
Confession.

He tells three, but
is ashamed of the other.

He comes out
with five.

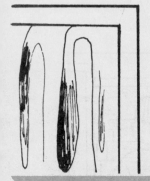

And no matter how often John goes to confession after this, no sin will ever be forgiven until he tells the one he deliberately left out. As often as he goes to confession without telling this sin, all his confessions will be bad. And if he goes to communion, this will be a sacrilege, too.

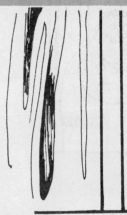
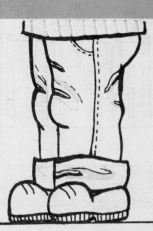

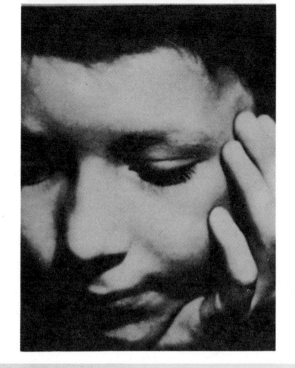

PRAYERS TO LEARN BY HEART

LORD'S PRAYER

Our Father, who art in heaven, hallowed be thy name; thy kingdom come; thy will be done on earth as it is in heaven. Give us this day our daily bread; and forgive us our trespasses as we forgive those who trespass against us; and lead us not into temptation, but deliver us from evil. Amen.

GLORY BE

Glory be to the Father, and to the Son, and to the Holy Spirit. As it was in the beginning, is now, and ever shall be, world without end. Amen.

HAIL MARY

Hail, Mary, full of grace, the Lord is with thee; blessed art thou among women, and blessed is the fruit of thy womb, Jesus. Holy Mary, Mother of God, pray for us sinners, now and at the hour of our death. Amen.

TO THE GUARDIAN ANGEL

*Angel of God, my guardian dear,
To whom his love commits me here;
Ever this day be at my side,
To light and guard, to rule and guide, Amen.*